God, I Know You Are There!
By
LaRita S. Smith

Illustrations by Jala McClain

©2023 LaRita S. Smith

God, I Know You Are There!

Written By LaRita S. Smith
Illustrations by Jala McClain
Edited by Joyce Lomax

No part of this publication may be reproduced, stored in a retrieval system, or transmitted in any form or by any means, electronic, mechanical, photocopying, recording, or otherwise, without written permission of the author. For information regarding permission, contact LaRita S. Smith at
flinc2014@yahoo.com

ISBN: 9798873782529

Copyright© 2023 by LaRita S. Smith. Independently published.
All rights reserved. Printed in the U.S.A
Back cover author photograph by Lauren Maebane

This book is dedicated to all God's children.

Train up a child in the way he (she) should go, and when he(she) is old, he (she) will not depart from it. Proverbs 22:6 KJV

Acknowledgments

First, I give honor God for His grace and mercy. I am grateful for the gifts He has bestowed upon me. I pray that He uses me as a vessel to inspire others to walk in their purpose.

To my mother, Alice Smith, thank you for instilling in me the importance of God and being a constant support. Although my father, William Smith, is no longer with me, he is forever in my heart. Thank you, Daddy, for all the advice and support you provided. You believed in me more than I believed in myself. Thank you both for your unwavering love.

To my entire family, there are too many to name individually. I love you all. I thank God for Blessing me to have you all in my life.

Special thanks to Crystal Hurtado, Lauren Maebane, Brenda Posley, Deja Maddox, Paris Banks, and Edna Meadors for all of the prayers, encouragement and advice given during my writing process.

Introduction

I wrote this book as a special message to parents and children. It is important that children are provided with a healthy and solid spiritual foundation. Introducing them to God during their formative years will lead them to a lifelong connection with Him. Children should know that God loves us; all He wants is for us to love Him too.

This book is not a teaching reference; however, I hope it will enlighten little listeners and show them that they are not too young to know God or feel His love.

God, I Know You Are There!

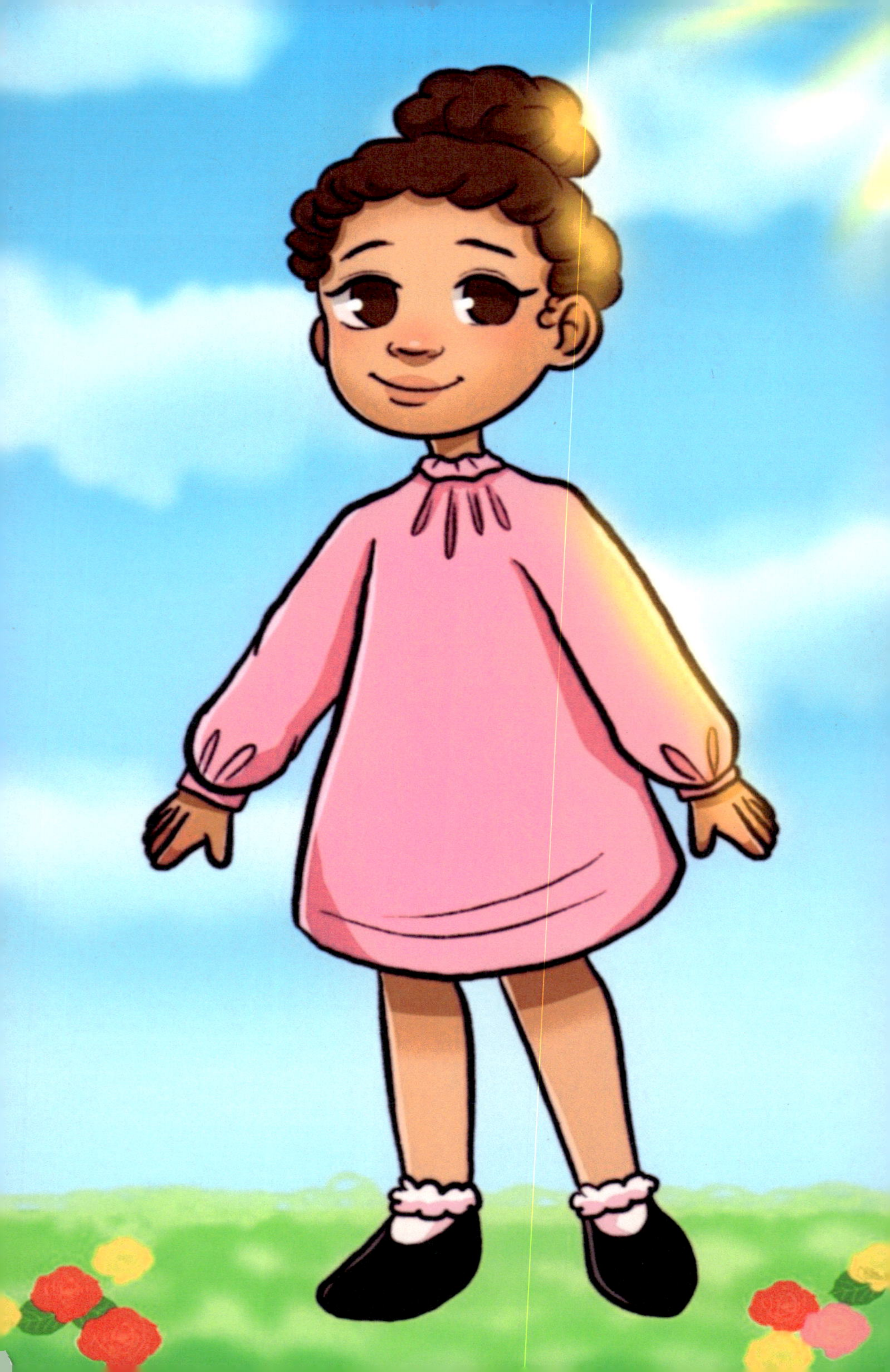

My name is Brea, and I am five years old. My parents told me that someone loves me. They say He lives beyond the skies and that I am a beautiful sight in His eyes.

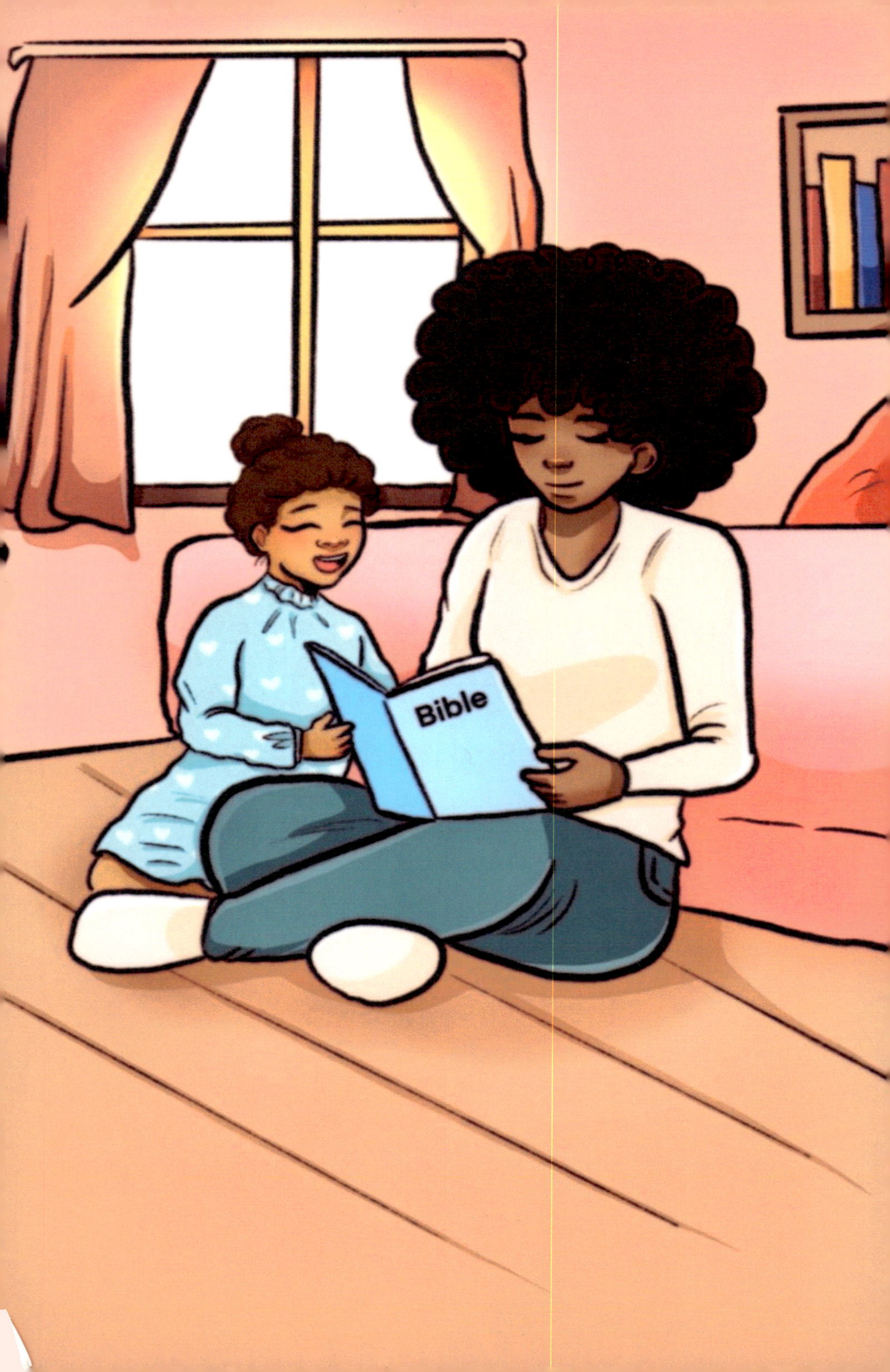
Bible

Mommy reads to me from a special book called the bible. She says that it is for both young and old. She says it is the most incredible story ever told.

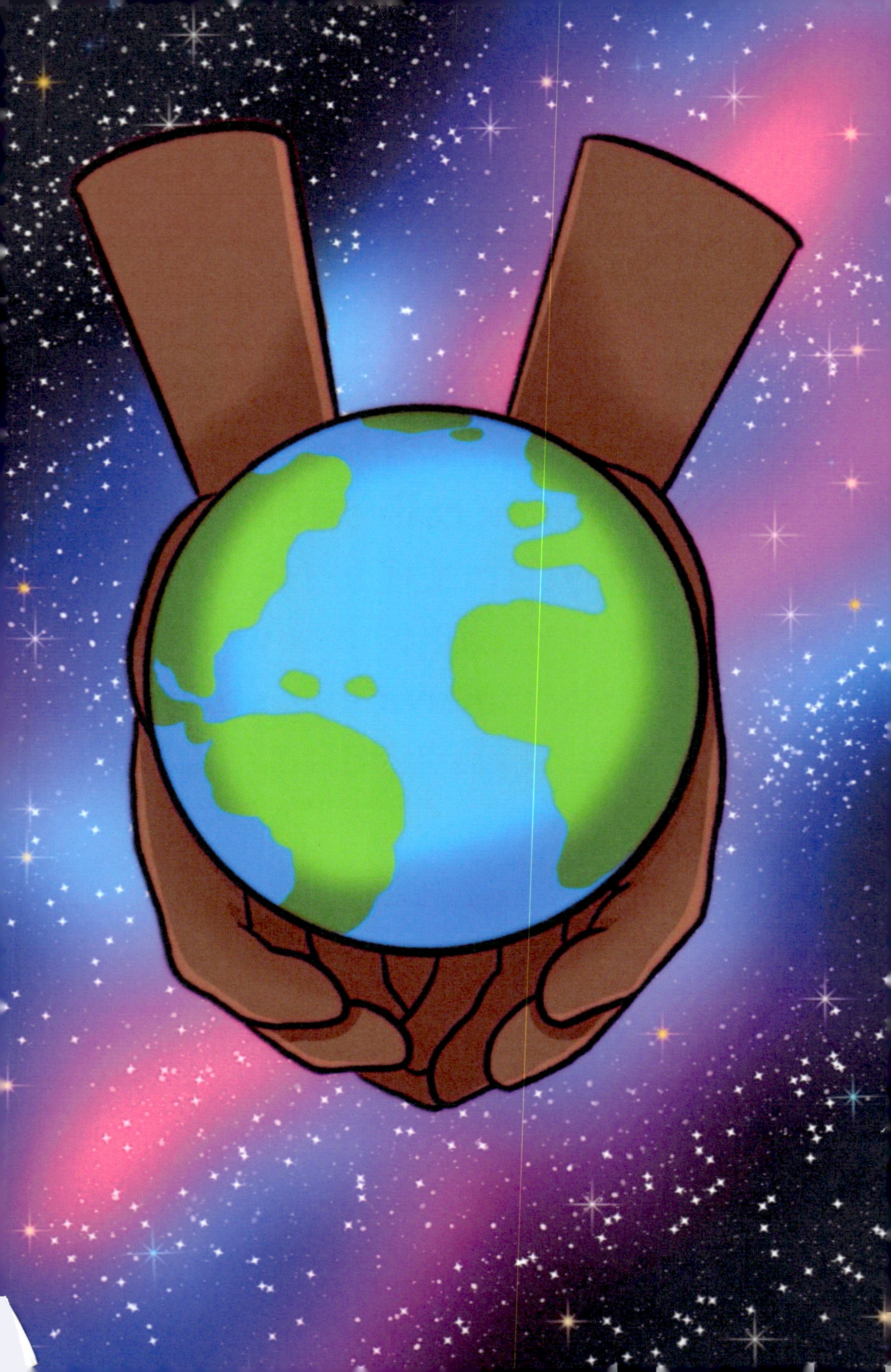

First God created heaven and earth. Then He made the moon, the stars and whole universe.

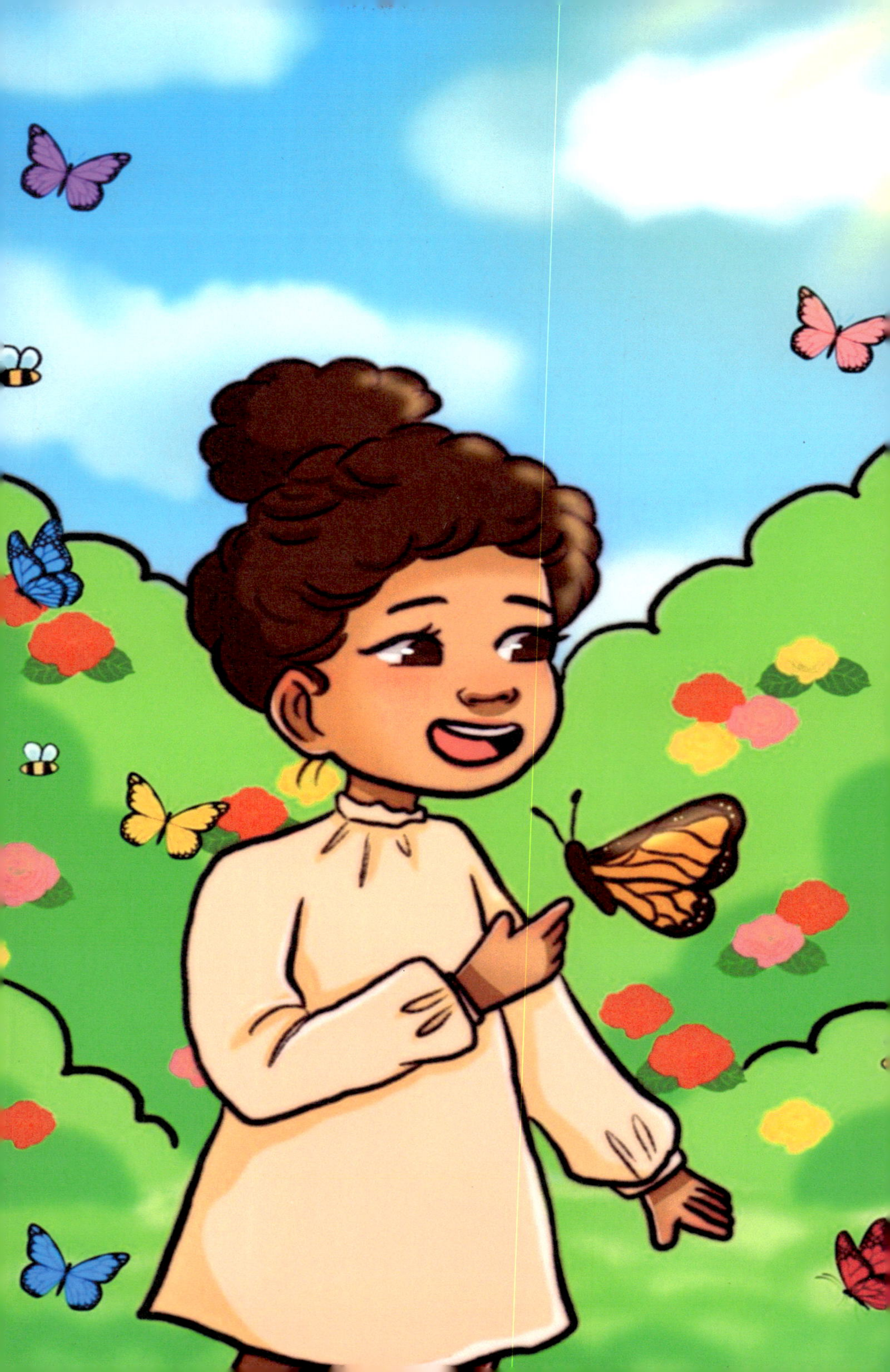

God created the flowers, the trees, the birds, and the bees. It was He who made the oceans and the seas. But best of all, He created you and me!

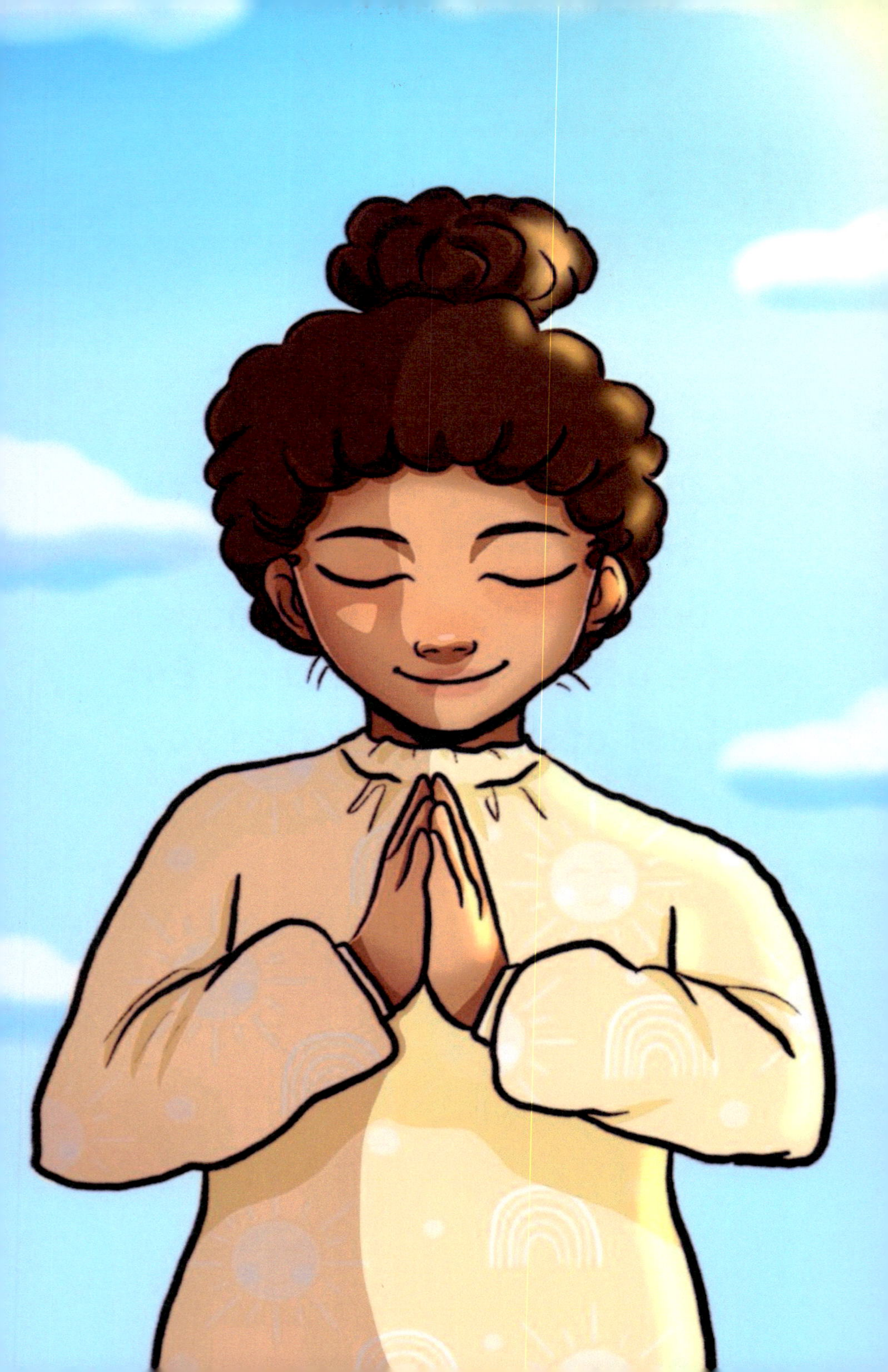

My parents say as I get older, I will understand that we are all part of God's divine plan.

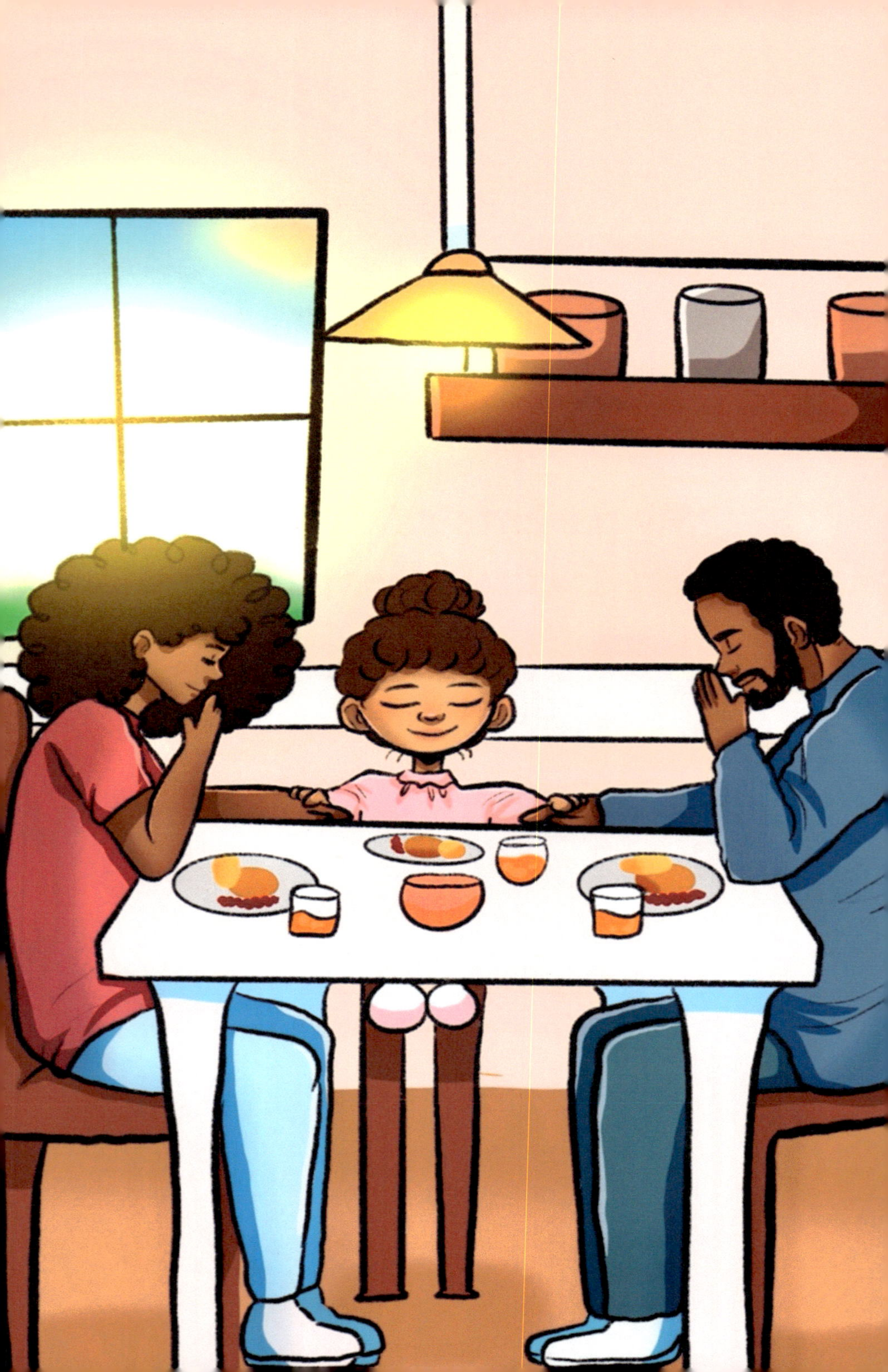

With closed eyes and held hands; we bow our heads to thank God for our food, "Amen"!

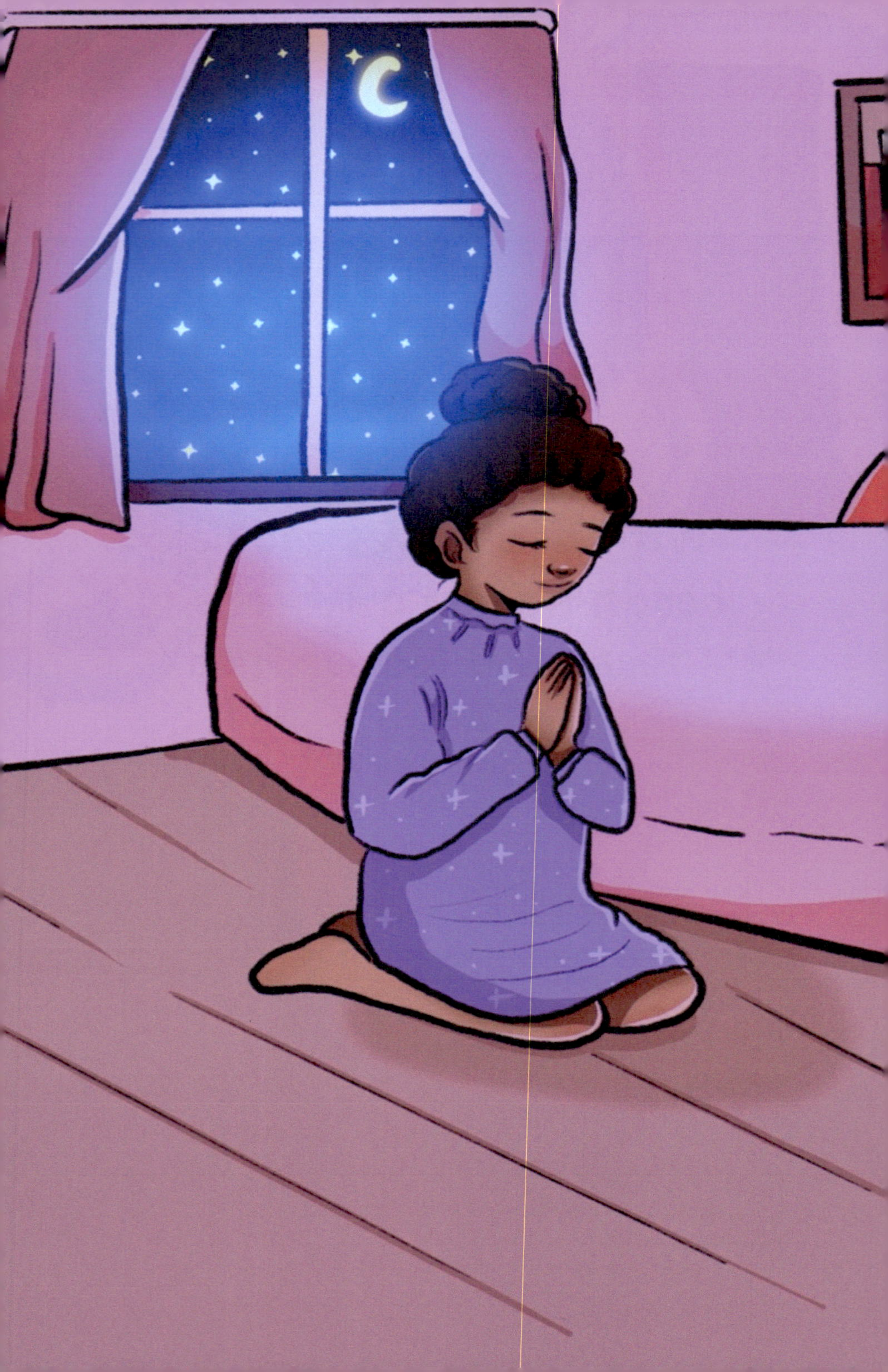

I say my prayers every night.
When I hear God's whisper,
I know everything is going to
be all right.

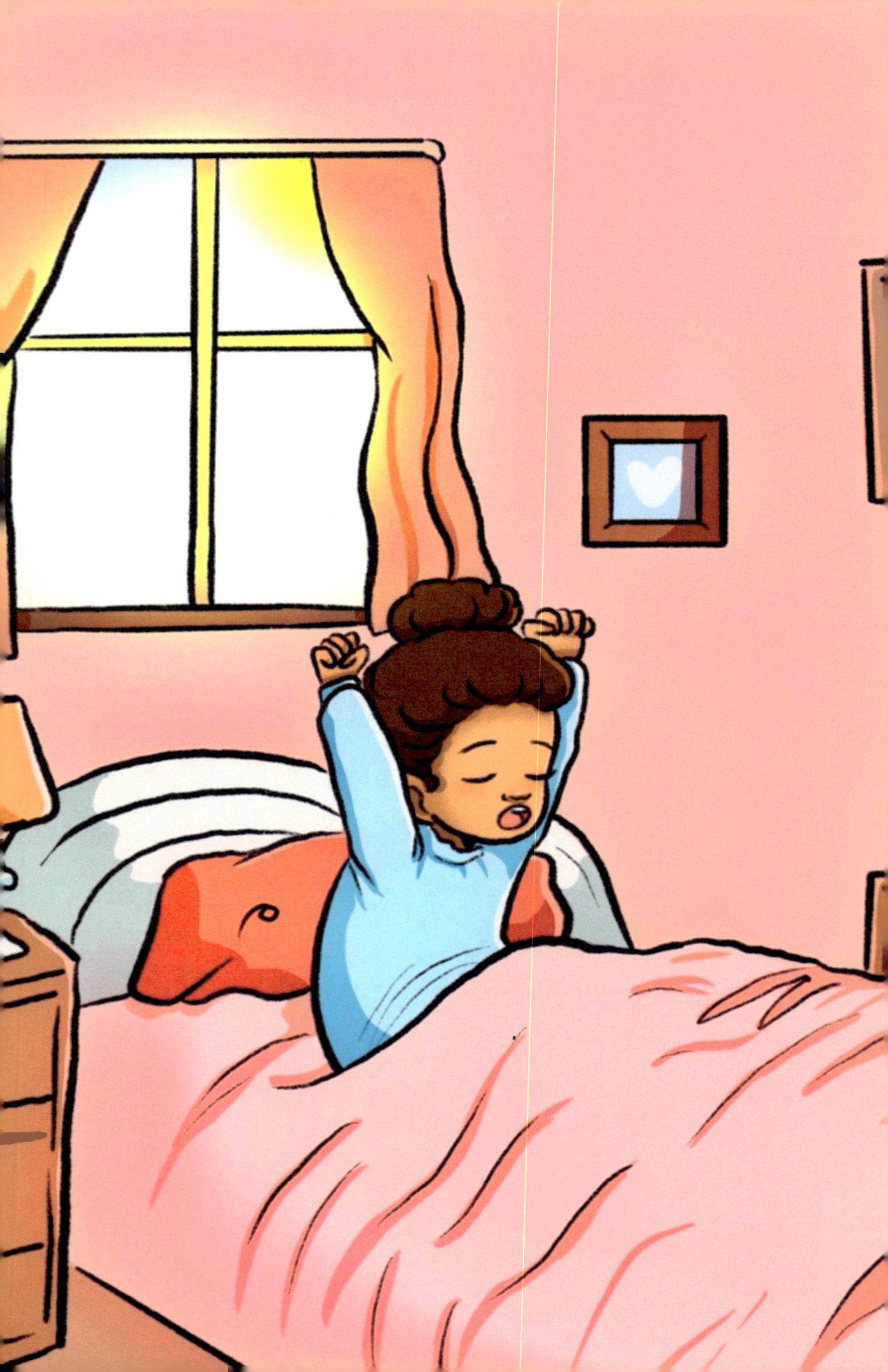

Every morning, when I wake,
I thank God for letting me
see a brand-new day!

Yahweh

El Shaddai

Elohim

Adonai

God our Father goes by many names... Whatever you choose to call him. He will answer just the same.

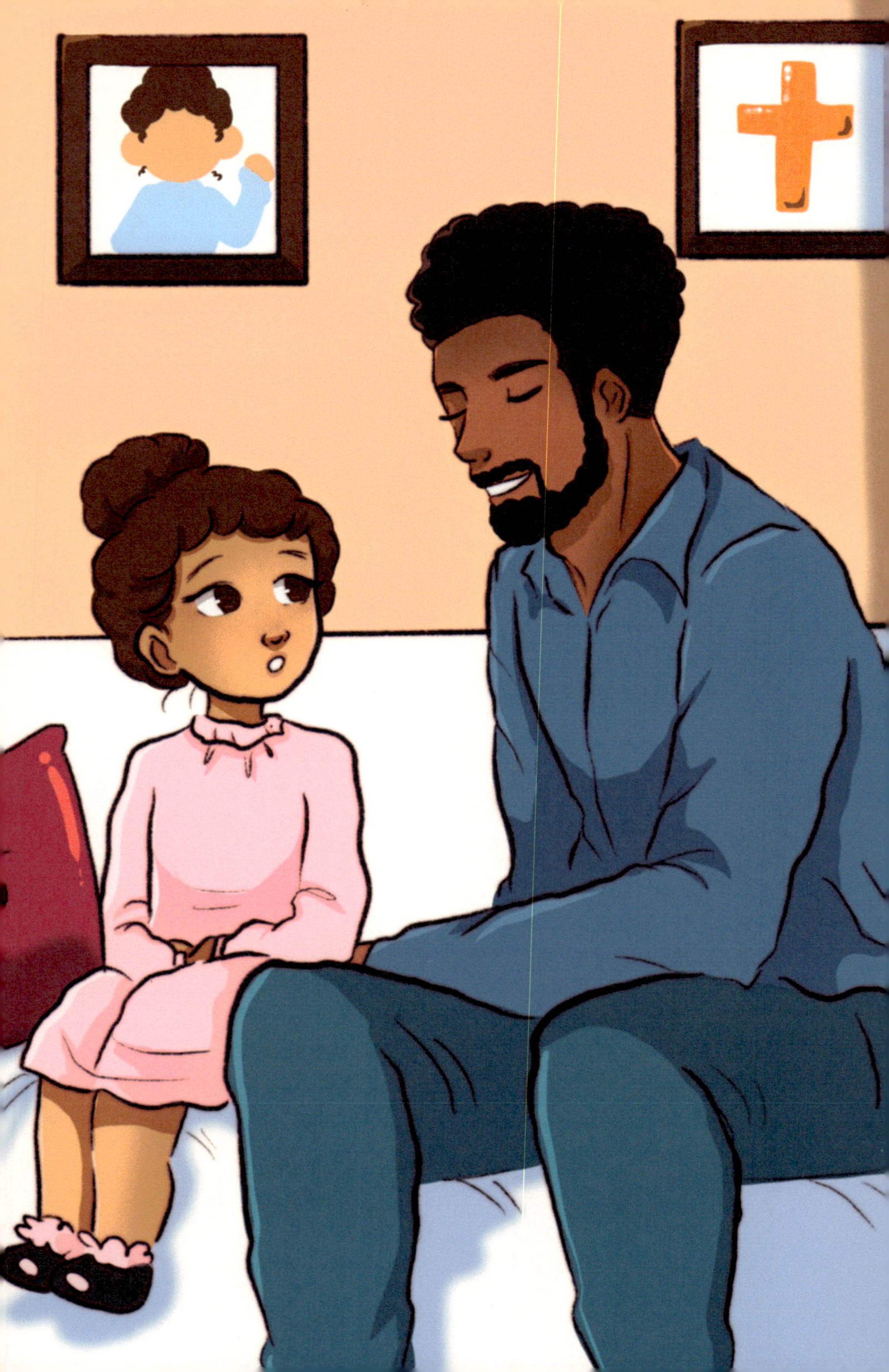

Daddy says the world was and is still full of sin, but God loves us so much. He made a way for us to see Him again.

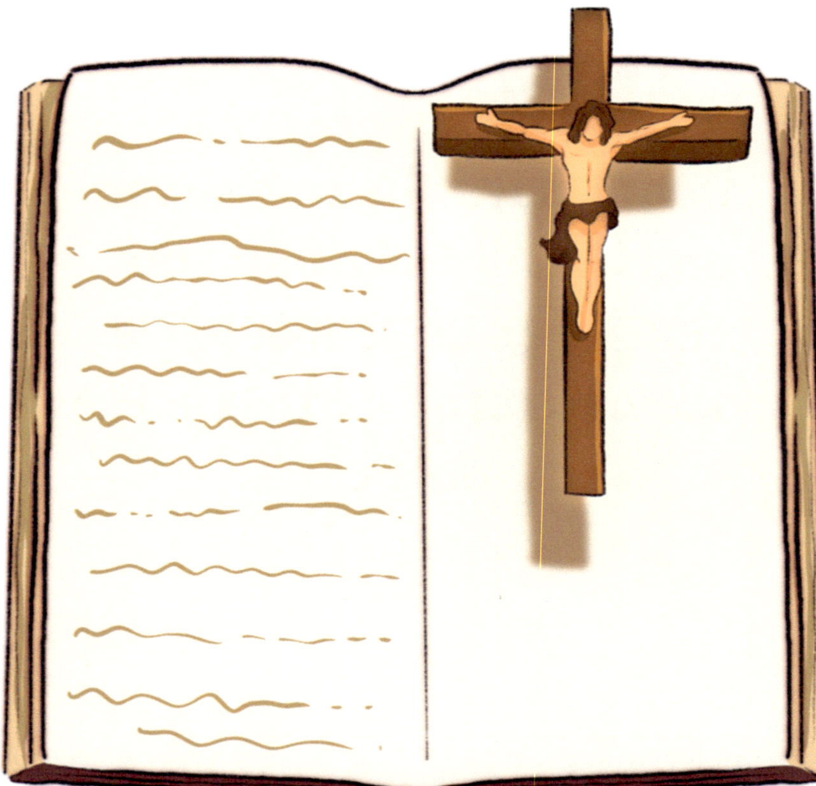

God sent His Son Jesus, who died on the cross so we wouldn't be lost. He gave His life freely so that we could live eternally.

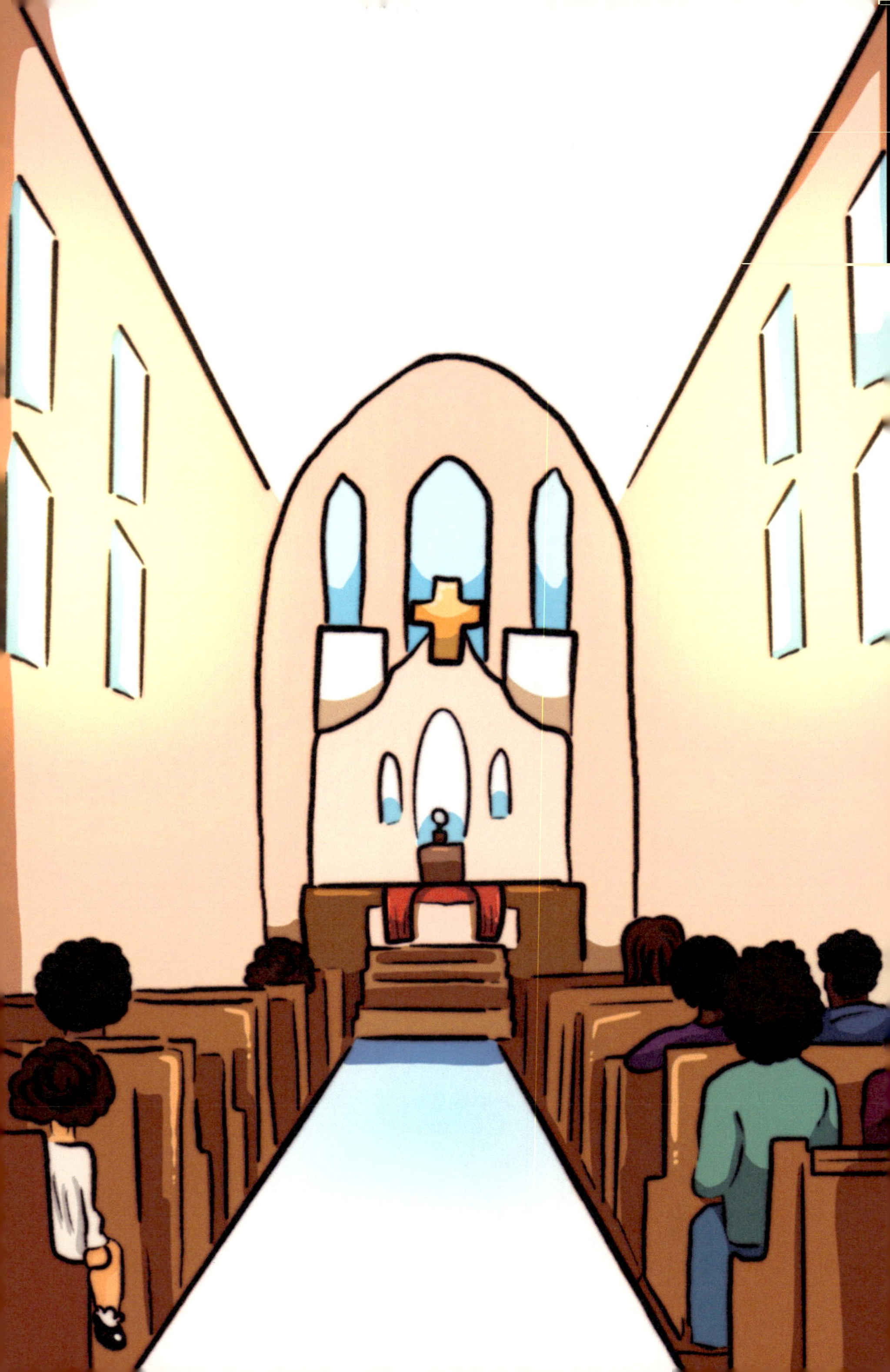

My family goes to God's house. It's called a church. Some have crosses, and others have steeples, inside ours, there are many people.

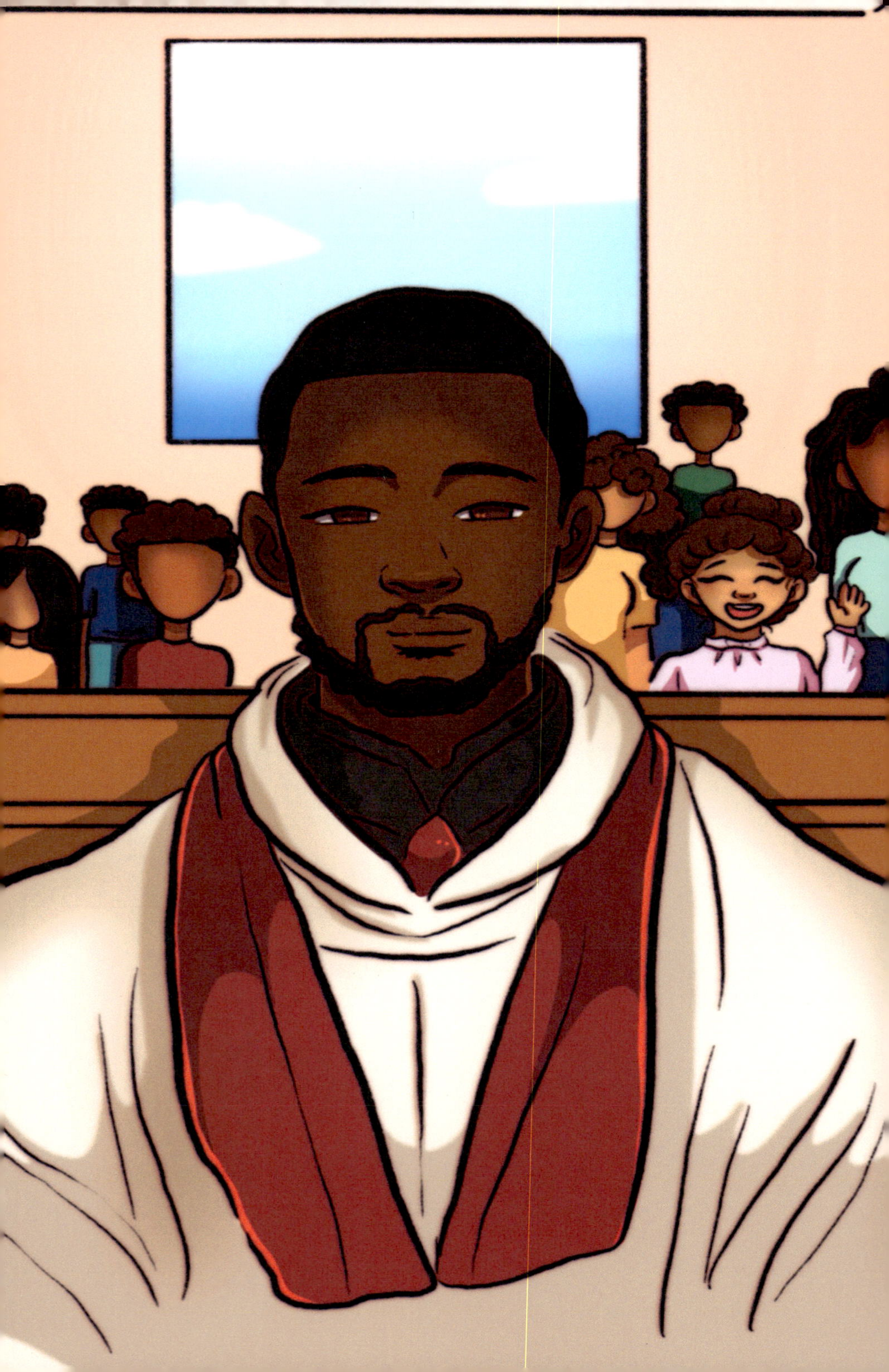

Each time I go, I learn something new. One thing I know and believe to be true; God will never stop loving me or you!

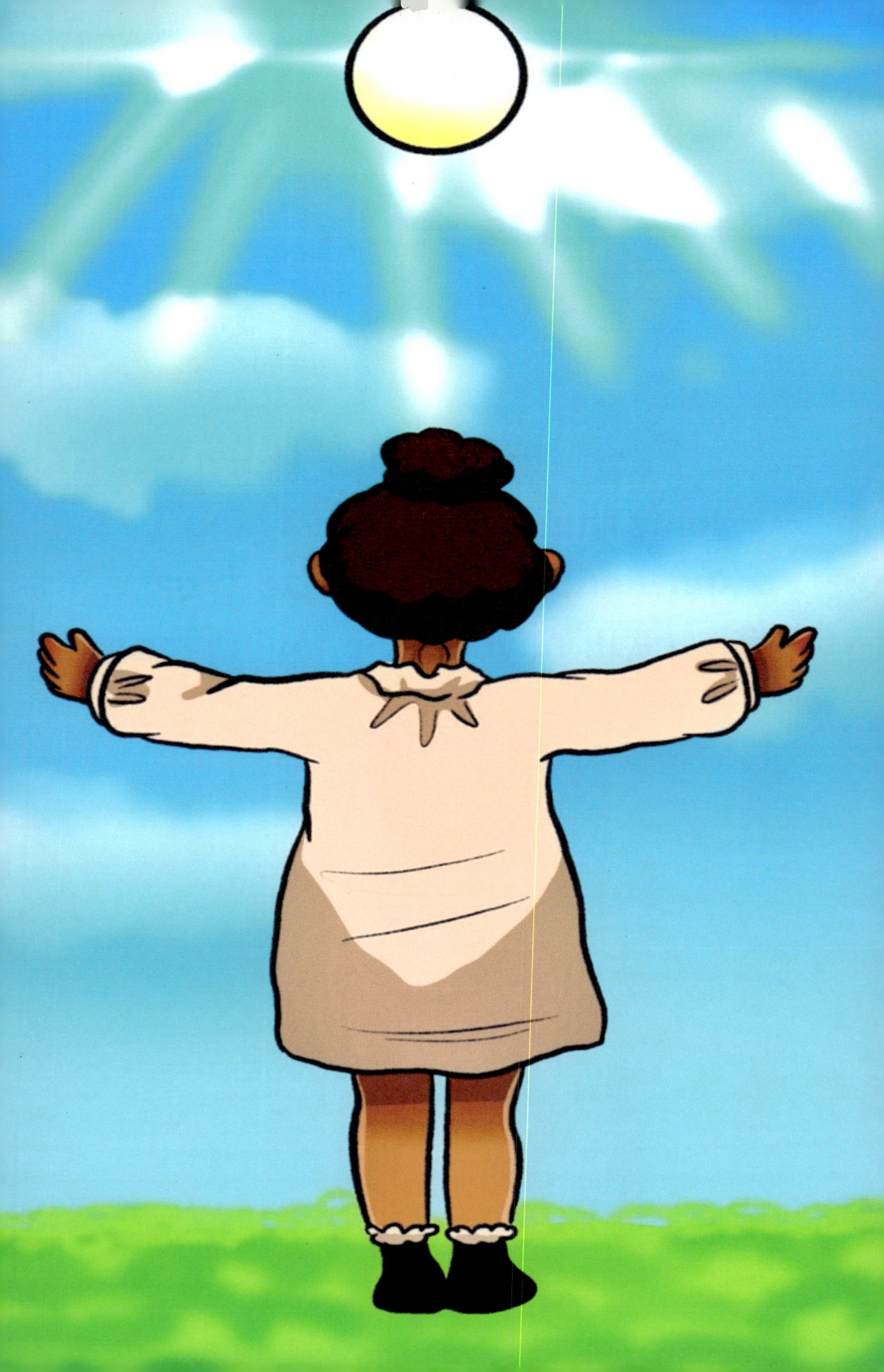

He is a ray of light, a bright beam in the sky. Sometimes, I can feel Him, even when I don't try. I bathe in the warmth that comes from the sun. It must be God because I feel surrounded by Love.

Made in the USA
Columbia, SC
19 February 2024